Furnished Rooms

Emanuel Carnevali

Edited and with an Afterword
by
Dennis Barone

Library of Congress Cataloguing-in-Publication Data

Carnevali, Emanuel.
Furnished rooms / Emanuel Carnevali ; edited and with an afterword
by Dennis Barone.
   p. cm. -- (VIA folios ; 43)
ISBN 1-884419-83-6 (alk. paper)
1. Italian-Americans--Poetry. I. Barone, Dennis. II. Title.

PS3505.A72752F87 2006
811'.52--dc22

2006043066

Printed in the United States.

Published by
BORDIGHERA PRESS
John D. Calandra Italian American Institute
25 W. 43rd Street, 17th Floor
New York, NY 10036

VIA FOLIOS 43
ISBN 1-884419-83-6

Table of Contents

The Book of Job Junior

*T*he faith that is in me and upholds this attempt of
mine – to say something about art from the artist's
and not the critic's standpoint – is worried into activity by
a great quantity of nagging little facts which merge into
this relevant one; ours are times of categorization, classifi-
cation, specialization.

In the beginning, Psyche was something of a light, agile
and naïf Greek myth, but now we have psychology, psycho-
analysis, psychiatry, psychic sciences, patho-psychology, patho-
pathology, subliminal selves, un-conscious, sub-conscious, hyper-
conscious, etc.

In the beginning a man grunted, "I am hungry," and
sat in ambush for the first saurian that happened along. Now,
there is socialism, bolshevism, capitalism, surplus theories,
submerged tenth, Italian table d'hotes, Mr. Fletcher, cafete-
rias.

In the beginning there was a lonely Phidias that made
statues and hardly knew, if at all, why or wherefore. Now
every irreverent mongrel who lifts his hind leg to leave a
desecration of ink on clean paper talks of technique.

We have come to times of specialization. Now one is
never through improving in any specialties, no specialist is
ever sufficiently specialized; so, my hopes to become a
successful specialist of whatever kind have all gone. I have
no sinews, no patience and no temperament fit for endless
work with far and dubious results; and, I will say, I have
no taste for boredom and I fear that an unbeautiful occupa-
tion is useless, nay, harmful, and sacrilegious toward Life.

So, I am neither an expert, nor a specialist. I have not
read extraordinarily much, and I don't know too many

languages, although I am not as ignorant as the typical American intellectual; I say I am an artist because if I cannot find a wider, less definite term; and because if I should tell you that I am a man, nothing more or less, you would smile and not understand.

The artist is no specialist. The artist is not an expert worker, a craftsman, a technician, he belongs nowhere because he belongs everywhere, he knows nothing because he knows everything; he is not a judge, not a scholar, not a king, not a captain, not a god, not a worker, not a lover – because he knows better, because he is a MAN and judge, scholar, king, captain, god, worker, lover – these are words that express a more definite and narrower and "more specific" concept than the concept, MAN.

Now, questions that are often put to artists and critics, such as, What is Art? What is an Artist? show that the questioners have in mind that the artist is something definite, something "special." I have often been told that some of my bad habits were effects of my artistic temperament. A lady once excused me for being sincere to her by saying, Yours is an artistic temperament. That is the point; artists are excused for being such, they are forgiven their loafing, their incorrigible laziness, and the fault is blamed on their artistic temperament. When it is no longer proper to excuse them, they are definitely placed in a remote part of the world of human creatures and thought of and dealt with as a specialty, one of the many varieties of homo sapiens. Thus the world goes on unhindered, making of our tangled and minute sophistication a soft bed for its rolling.

The voice of the people says: the artist is a specialist who attains perfect craftsmanship by the perusal of a certain technique. Of course, some obvious things would be left out of such an explanation; but the voice of the people says that they are easily stuffed in again. In fact, if I ask,

2

How about the social value of art? the voice of the people promptly answers, that since every specialization is the effect of certain social conditions it has therefore a bearing upon social conditions. And so on and so on, and you will not find a single person who has not one or two answers of the kind ready. The strange fact is that almost everyone who is at all concerned knows something or everything about art. It is only the artists who do not know. It is but natural that people who are not artists express an opinion on art with infinite more facility than the artist himself; to whom every sorrowing moment of every sorrowing day brings a new concept of art; and every tiny joy that flutters by him a new idea of art, a totally new idea; to whom what art is, and whether art is, is a matter of life and death, or, if you don't like the turgid phrase, a matter of sanity or insanity; witness Schumann, Blake, Maupassant, Strindberg, Verhaeren.

Did a man ever know what art is? Not know, but sense it, men surely did. And all their lives and every minute of their lives, were spent in saying it. A work of art is. It is the only human manifestation that is exclusively, violently, intolerantly itself and nothing else ... the only human manifestation that can define its existence in terms of its sheer being; that is what an artist, Giovanni Papini, means when he says that "art is the only depositor of the Absolute." One cannot say what art is otherwise than by producing a work of art. A work of art is an attempt to say what art is, its only scope is that. If it is art and you understand it then you will have gone as far as its maker in his attempt to know what art is, and, in that particular contemplative moment, no farther. And do you not think it gullible to try to surpass such a contemplative moment by means of that benignant, imbecile unconcern that you assume when you say; art is this, art is that.... Only a mood, your own, personal, individual, holy mood will give you a glimpse or more than a glimpse into the comprehension of art. Spingarn, the disciple of Croce, and Croce, the disciple of Hegel, have said something about this, about Creative Criticism, about the aesthetic moment of Criticism.

Self-limitation is self-amputation, self-warping. Let us call it two movements, the ebb and the flow. One the artistic movement, the flow. The other, the unartistic movement, the ebb. Men defend themselves, hide, protect themselves, lie – all things of the ebb, ripples sliding down in the abyss of death and hell. Cynicism, unbelief, crime, tragedy, dumbness, ugliness, things which need to defend themselves and things of self-defense, things of cowering self-preservation, ripples of the ebb. Anything is acceptable as long as it shelters us, everything is longed for, prayed for, which protects us; love for our shames and needs, for our failures, for comfort; all that which remedies, all that which reforms, all that which affords or purveys forgetfulness – these are all symbols of the tremendous universal retreat, retreat to shelter and forgetfulness – all symbols of the ebb – symbols of fear, which rivets religion in men's chests. Sometime the fear accumulates, the shelters are too crowded; then revolutions and wars happen, explosions.

The ebb, all the brief ineffectual attempts – all the provisoriness of the world – because people are hurried – death hunts them – and so, quickly, they build houses that are ugly, withstand like sullen oxen all the unbearable ugliness of a city like Chicago, because they are not out to live, not out to conquer, they are out in spite of themselves – for these men are conscious of one thing only, that they are in the ebb of the world. Thus they undergo. They know one thing, that they must undergo, life being extraneous to them; life is therefore, something unknown and fearful, and when they make a God, he symbolizes Life to them, a fearful thing. Sometimes they elevate the public to the

4

height of a God and they do so to put fear into the hearts of the enemies of the public.

But I am aware that I am now vaguely touching the tremendous sinews of what we indifferently call Art.

For the ebbing sensations are not to be acknowledged – they defend themselves from sensations, sometimes killing them, sometimes benumbing them, but nearly always by taking care of them, by means of classification and specialization. You can then say this: Art is the happy acknowledgment of sensation. To acknowledge a sensation means not to fear truth. And there cannot be another meaning to the word truth but this, life. To live is to know truth. Or rather, to sense it, for nothing is knowable in the way philosophers understand the word knowable. Only the senses are our interpreters, our body is the vessel that bears truth, our body is the wireless receiving station of the universe. When a mood reigns, then the senses know truth – when it is an artistic mood, that is, a complete mood, then all the senses are mobilized, a perfect synthesis happens, all truth is then revealed. The body is a part of the infinite, moved in the spasm of the infinite. But again, definitions and definitions! There must be some use in them too, must there not? I would, however, rather sense the two opposite forces, for they surely exist, the ugly and the beautiful and say why I want to be the latter force. I say to have a mood is to live. If a mood comprehends life then it comprehends all life, then it is a symbol of all life symbol, meaning intrinsic part of a whole, glimpse of the marvelous completeness. Within the moods all things are connected, follow one another harmoniously and since life is motion, follow one another in perfect motion – thus we come to it, harmony and rhythm. Harmony is in a mood when no part of the man is struggling against any other part, when a man is a complete being, when he lives, when he is a sign of all life – and to be one thing, one whole, in a world as ours, a world of ugliness, means to will, means to will liberation, means to be a motion upward and away from – thus I proclaim: a poem today must be one single, absolute, definite will.

And then there is only one ugliness, lack of harmony – which means lie. A man can lie in one way only – to his own will. When a man lies, no harmony is in him, he's unbeautiful. Every ugliness is a self-contradictory contradiction. Every beauty is an absolute will. Ugliness means tragedy, immorality self-murdering hunger, brief breath of Death, I cannot say it. But try to guess. I do not condemn the snout of Mr. McCabe because it does not please me, but because it does not please him. I do not loathe his eyes because they are not in harmony with my faith in eyes, but because the man who has those eyes will know that there are things he must not look at, that he may not dare, that he may not will – and to prove what I say, well what does McCabe look like? What is he? Here the poem comes in, here the work of art comes in which describes McCabe. The artist takes the lines of the face, the lumps of flesh in McCabe and to feel, to conceive McCabe's lines he must have a conception of pure lines. He inevitably does compare them with pure lines. Lines he has seen. What lines? Lines he has seen and everybody sees. Aboriginal, unwarped, beautiful lines. Where has he seen them? Everywhere, where everybody sees them. Just as McCabe sees them. When McCabe refuses to look at them and shuts his eyes – there his darkness begins, there his fear begins. McCabe will invent for himself perverted lines, make his face a twist and uphold and proclaim the twist – then his lie will begin, and his tragedy. And why the tragedy? Because if it is to himself that he lies, that part of him which is lying, KNOWS THE TRUTH. Art is when a man tells the truth to himself. If the life of artists is tragic it is because he

6

has TO TELL ALOUD the truth to defeat a lie – a lie which is also, of course, fatally, inevitably, his own lie.

Morals, economics, anthropology, law, commerce, set rules slowly shifting backward until an upheaval shakes them down the shoulders of the world. It is in the face of men that you will see them denied, it is, more than ever, in everything everybody needs and the way everybody would go about getting it, that they are denied: air, sunlight, food, clothes, speech. Who has perfectly breathed? Who has been a perfect thing in the sunlight, and known it and never denied that sun-proclaimed truth, that sunlit image and posture? Who has known his clothes and known why he has put them on in the morning? Who has dressed himself truly? What clothes are true to a man?

Until achieved, perfections must be related. There shall be artists and people who are not artists. I have said that so often that I am afraid it is untrue by this time. But let us see.

To understand means to personify. An artistic image is an assimilation, a personification, a bringing of all human values to understand one human value. Those who do not understand do so because they do not want to. Brain is nothing, brain does not exist. Brain is the center which could not exist without the circumference. And the circumference is our own nerves. And our nerves could not be without our flesh. We are a whole. He who does not understand has an unbeautiful body which seeks to forget itself, which seeks darkness. He who does not understand has shut the doors of his body because ... because he had to, because light hurt him – rather, because he thought he had to, because he did not know that LIGHT ALWAYS HURTS, always, and that we must be hurt, nowadays, in 1921, because it is late, because we are overgrown, because evidently our palaces and our houses are the dressed-over remains of a time in which palaces and houses were something to look at, WERE. Nowadays, if a poem does not hurt, if it does not bring before our eyes the skull of our own skeleton – it is not a poem, it is not art.

To understand means to personify. The artist acknowledges your ugliness as his own; therefore, Schumann goes crazy, therefore, Strindberg goes crazy; therefore Christ fails. The artist is an inseparable limb of an immense body – the world. You would call him a specialist because YOU WISH TO AMPUTATE THAT LIMB. He also apologizes, he alone excuses himself, he alone begs...because he yet may. The others do not apologize because they have lost hopes of being forgiven, the others do not beg because they are certain no one will give. Therefore, they kill and steal, therefore, they make laws and enforce them, therefore, they proclaim such weird sinister lies as HONOR, HONESTY, RESPECT, PATRIOTISM, SOCIALISM, etc. No one of them believes them. No one ever believes in a lie. What happens then? They draw no happiness thereof. But their concern is no longer to believe in them, but to make their neighbor believe in them. Those things are pit-falls for the neighbor. And the neighbor falls. And the neighbor has also so prepared such pitfalls; so the neighbor's neighbor falls in, too. And they have not as yet found that it is a most ridiculous affair.

All is taken care of, which means fettered, silenced because it cannot be let to speak. If it would be let to speak, there would be need of ears to listen to it, and that would make them stop ... frozen by the voice. And as they are being chased by Death they are afraid to stop. What, what would happen if the voice of all was heard?

Everybody would come down to the street, and the streets would be crowded with persons going nowhere. Every two eyes that would meet two other eyes would tell frightful things. So, awful hatreds would be kindled, awful desires would lick and lap the bodies of those whom the eyes would see. Everybody then would see the houses, looming like fate, with terrible feet planted irrevocably in the belly of the sorrowing earth. And it would be too late then to say, "I understand your voice, I am going to listen to it and my life will be changed, my life will be must be, an echo to your voice." And as it would be too late, they would not say a word, but they would know that only death remains for them. For it is too late to make for the secret ambushing, for the underhanded deception for having lied to everybody. And then, and then, oh, maybe they'd kill and kill, and they'd destroy the houses...or maybe they would beg of their children to forgive them and forget them ... to forgive them. And the children who are all artists, would say: "We haven't the time. We must be taking care of ourselves. We must be ridding ourselves of your heredity." So they'd all go to die, in corners, like dogs, unknown, unacknowledged, unidentified. And in years the houses would cave in over their ashes.

You see, this is hardly a supposition. This is more or less what really happens. The drama is always in motion. Art is in the world. Art exists always.

Form. Form is one and universal. There is but man and the universe that is a necessary premise. Man understands form only when he is form. When he is swept by an emotion into form and becomes the intrinsic part of form. It is form which assimilates the artist.

Those whom Form does not acknowledge, those who would try not to acknowledge form, are the faceless. They are faceless in their own eyes, not in the artist's eyes, because they do not escape form. They are called the damned, the misshapen, the ugly, the fools.

Certainly since they are repetitions, Blake, Nietzsche, Dostoievsky, Shelley, William Williams, Waldo Frank, truth does not become old and die, as is the fad to say nowadays. Christ's words are as true now as they ever were.

But I started out to explain, that is, to compromise, not to make art. Compromise with those of you who ask what art is, then tell one Art is one plus one equals two. There is nothing magnificent and nothing patronizing in my attitude. It is for my own sake that I wanted to compromise.

But our concern then? Is it to repeat? No. Our concern should be to liberate this moment, this present moment from its frightful tangle. To strive toward the form of this moment. What is its form? A poem from me to you, that would be it. Can I recite now a poem?

There has not been only art. There has been Nietzsche also. At moments I deny art, I do not believe in the possibility of a poem. Moments like these are real, although no poem exists. They are moments in which I am out among the people I object to, out to try to know them, out to try to know where I stand among them. This speech of mine may be as abject self-defense as yours is when you attempt to place the artist somewhere OUTSIDE of you. I, in fact, think it is. Acknowledge that and proceed.

Oh, let me tell you, there may have been a Balzac or a Dostoievsky, but today an artist is an awful scream from the dry, musty throats of the earth; today is a time of death and end and hurry, and Bill Williams dances better than Romain Rolland the dance, macabre and wonderful, of today. All the old truths are true today, too, but the world has gone ahead without hearing them. So it is quite appropriate that a sneer for the great big truths is setting on mother earth's face. Today wants new approaches, new absurdities, new crazes, new dances, new dislocations. Today does not want truth. Let the artist retire to his damn infinite and let him keep quiet. Let him connive with his pure beauty, but we are hungry, and the time has come when the artists, or call them what you please, are yelling for food. Food, food, food. They are becoming afraid, too. They are in with the rest, everybody. They are facing the same death, and they must fight it out. A poem nowadays cannot be if it isn't violent. All the ludicrous stunts, all the risible attempts, all the undignified exhibitions are allowed and encouraged, to be allowed and encouraged. But the old stale contemplation, pure art – it is sitting and it has not noticed that the world has gone away, away, away for good, never to come back. Here we are, you and I. This is the big situation, the crucial point. There is one thing for me to do, if I want to live in your world. Make you acknowledge me. Make you understand me. From now on, every work of art shall be a talk to the people. Call it compromise, if you will, I thought myself of that word. Today wants pragmatic works. Visions are risible. It wants a will. It wants moralities, stated with more efficiency than they have heretofore been stated with. For the only signs of life, the artists are dying. And I, for one, do not want to die. And it depends on you whether I do or not, that means, it depends on how much and how well I speak to you. Your cities are impossible, the breath of our cities is the breath of a drunkard the morning after; the food in your cities poisons me; your theatres are too indecent for a person not thoroughly devoid of modesty. Either I die uselessly as so many other fools have, or something must be done. A coalition of the artists, a new religion, a universal prohibition forbidding ... everything that is now being sold, or something. The self-sufficient artists, God bless their cold feet, they may grunt about the infinite in their cozy sties. And I wish the solitaries achieved a more thorough dignity and that they'd quit publishing their works. It is America, this land without a physiognomy, this land of enemy aliens, this land of moving pictures and new republics and dill pickles. It is America. She wants no truth. She can't walk in the right road any longer; it is too late. She must take a

11

short cut and skip and stumble and bruise her knees in the brambles and go mad in the desperate race. Some countries have a culture. Culture is a room where people sit and talk quietly, friends who lawfully and conventionally meet to talk till not too late hours. But here a man must yell if he wants to be heard, and not heard by the people but heard by his very few friends. Yell like poor Bill Williams did in *Others*. Men here must go out at night, meet in the dark and dodge policemen. That is dignity, today. Or that isn't dignity. That is strength. Well that is the strength of dying men.

You're right, this is an attitude, and I too am sick of it. It's a craze. But at any rate it is a mood. And it continues. It is in me. So you'll have more of it.

It is a fight against fools. It is a fight similar to the fools' fight for self-preservation, for shelter. It is a fight, I need this release:

Good Lord, you have committed enough crimes! What? Dante was chased like a homeless dog from one town to another, he mustered you all down into hell, he called Italy

> not a city woman
> but a whore

and you ask whether art is a delicate way of scratching one's self or a new Parisian rouge for bleached lips. Shakespeare sent desperate Hamlet to exhibit his awful brain tangle, puffed him full with the rage of all the storm winds, made him nasty and brutal with as sweet a wench as Ophelia, encouraged him to end it all with a mighty butchery, and you ask whether criticism is the exclusive concern of baldheaded professors or a way to appreciate Mary Roberts Rinehart. Criticism is hellfire, death and destruction, war and revolution and all the fun there is in rockets and gas bombs and smoke-screens and camouflage, butchery and a dance macabre of ghosts, of murdered kings and princes gone mad withal, that's what criticism is. William Blake stuttered and stuttered until he went insane, went insane for the sake of showing you how he could stick to it (because his insanity was out of punctilio) and you ask whether rhymed poems are better than free verse ones, and how I like Sara Teasdale. Rimbaud threw it all out in cataracts of gold and emerald and ruby and was done for at twenty and you ask what symbolism is. Symbolism is the sinister will to get out of the filth you live in, that's what it is.

It is your turn to do something. Begin today. You have never been original. Do something for God's sake; refuse to be a silly repetition. Begin today. I don't say, leave us alone. I don't say, leave me alone. We don't want that. Or—as there are some artists around, and they may resent that WE—I don't want that. I say, go look at your face before you speak to me, who am always standing before mirrors. Go wash your hands before you touch me. I don't want you to believe me. Why should you believe me? I said nothing, I screamed, for I'm drunk with the alcohol no prohibition can suppress, alcohol of perdition and damnation, which one drinks as he breathes in your horrible streets. Believe in yourself. Be definite toward me. It is years and years that the artists have defined their attitude toward you, now define your attitude toward the artists. Toward me, here, beginning from now and hurry up. I have been studying your ways, I know quite a few of your tricks, but I haven't any desire to know them all, and I haven't the deadly patience of Sherwood Anderson. See, none of your tricks work. If you die, if you croak, if you burst, if you whither, it is not a matter of surprise anymore. It matters to the infinite perhaps, but Balzac and Dostoievsky took care of that transaction.

13

Aren't you ashamed of dying in the same way people used to die years and years ago? For God's sake, aren't you ashamed of repeating every day the mushy last scene of the Dame with the Camellias, and your muscular beaux are they not ashamed of their played-out stunts a la D'Artagnan, a la Cyrano De Bergerac, a la Jean Valjean. Read, read, read and learn what is stale. Seek newness. When an artist says there is nothing but the new he means – today one must not repeat the failure of Laforgue, the failure of Baudelaire, the failure of Christ. Failures have lost their romantic attractiveness. The world wants men who will dance even when they shall be leperish with all your leprosy. The infinite does acknowledge you and all your hackneyed deeds. That is probably Waldo Frank's opinion, and Sherwood Anderson's and Carl Sandburg's. They are mature men, they are big men also; they may be right. But here it isn't a matter of right or wrong; it's a fight. Truth, truth is an old witch, and let her ride on her broomstick. I'm out here with an old anger in me. Not for a poem, but with you, unclean with your way, using your ways, unclean with your touch. They have been slandering you, I want to talk to you the same way you'd talk to me, that's all. When I say you, I mean the public. My face is a reflection of yours, and as your face is a twisted yell of fear, so is my face a twisted yell of fear. Here we are, not you and I any more then, but we. Let us talk of ourselves then.

The Splendid Commonplace

DROLATIQUE-SERIEUX

Through the lowered awning's chink
The sun enters my room with the glad fury
Of a victorious dagger wielded by an adventurous child.
I smoke;
On the blade of the golden dagger
The smoke of my cigarette
Writhes, struggles, seems to wail and protest,
Then escapes, runs away, hurriedly, out of the window.
It meets the sun---
This blue, dream-fed smoke meets the sun.
The sun has no dream---
Perhaps it is Truth itself,
So beautiful!
Then it's wrong, very wrong,
To puff my dream in the radiant face of Truth?
Is it blasphemous, cowardly?
Is it to insult the Sun?

HIS MAJESTY THE LETTER-CARRIER

Half past seven in the morning
And the sun winks at me,
Half hidden by the last house of the street.
His long fingers
Scare away these trotting little men
Who rush westward from the east to their jobs.
Laughing, the sun pursues them...
Ah, there he is!
Who?... The letter-carrier, of course!
(What do you think I got up so early for?)
You never see him run —
He is so proud
Because he's got my happiness in that dirty bag:
He's got a kiss from my sweetheart,
Some money for me to buy some food,
And a white, nice collar.
That's why he's so conceited,
That's why he wants to show
That he doesn't know the sun is behind him,
That the laughing sun is behind him
Pushing him along to make him bring me my happiness;
A kiss from my sweetheart,
Some money to buy some food and a clean collar,
And a letter from an editor that says:
"You're a great poet, young man!"

Damn it! I guess he heard me raving about him:
He passed by my door and didn't even turn around.
What shall I do, what shall I do?

Oh, never mind — tomorrow, tomorrow!

IN THIS HOTEL

The headwaiter says:
"Nice day to-day!"
He smiles sentimentally.
The headwaiter says:
"It will rain to-day!"
He frowns gracefully.
Those are the greetings, every morning.
To every old lady,
And every old gent,
And every old rogue,
And every young couple –
To every guest.

And I, who do not sleep, who wait and watch for the dawn,
One day I would come down to the world
I would have a trumpet as powerful as the wind,
And I would trumpet out to the world
The splendid commonplace:
"Nice day to-day!"
And another day I would cry out in despair,

"It will rain to-day!"
For every old lady,
And every old gent,
And every old rogue,
And every young couple –
Are they not guests in this hotel,
Where the ceiling is the sky
And the floor is the earth,
And the rooms are the houses?

But I, I — this wretched, tired thing —
May I ask for a job
As headwaiter
Of this hotel?

COMMONPLACES

How Are You?

I wish that you all be well,
And that the sick ones of you get well;
I want a big, fresh, clean world.
Do you, too?
Is that what you mean
When you say:
"How do you do?"
"How do you feel?"

I Am Glad To See You

I am glad to see you:
My life still missed
One aspect;
And here you come
To fill the longing for you
That was in the breath of a sad hour.
I surely wanted to see you
For I greet you with words too plain to hide a lie:
"I am glad to see you."

The Day of Summer

To Waldo Frank

MORNING

How long ago was it
The dawn pleased Homer?
And Petrarca — was it among flowers
Dew-full, tearful for the love of the dawn,
That he sang his best song
For Laura?
Did the eyes of joy of Prince Paul Fort
See it well once,
And was it then that he
"Took pleasure in being a Frenchman?"
In New York,
These summer days,
It's a swollen-faced hour,
Sick with a monstrous cold,
Gasping with the death of an expectance.
Houses there
In a thick row
Militarily shut out the sky;
Another fence
In the east;
Over this one a shameful blush
Strives upward.

   Nevertheless I go to perform the ceremony
   Of purification — to wash myself . . .
   Oh, dear water . . . dear, dear soap . . .

Because I am poor
No ceremony will clean me;
In this crowded room
All the things touch me,

Soil me.
To start a day
Feeling dirty
Is to go to war
Unbelievingly.

A little happy pause here
For me to think of what I shall be doing in the day.

Now has the deep hot belly of the night
Given birth to noises.
The noises pass
Over me,
I lie
Insensible,
Under.
Work, milk, bread, clothes, potatoes, potatoes . . .
This is
The big
Beauty rumbling on.
Is this
The world's
Music forevermore?
This and the irrevocable peddlers
Who will come in an hour
To hurl loose:
"Pota-a-a-a-*t-o-u-s, yeh*-p-l-s, *waa-ry* meh-l-*n?*"
Little apocalyptic faces,
Faces of the end of all faces —
Are these the chief musicians?
Please, listen, I have a small, dear soul, and all I want

Is a noiseless beauty, any little thing, I was born
For a sylvan century, may I claim to be left alone? . . .
I will not even expect you to understand — only . . .

24

Under this, like a cold hating prostitute,
I lie
Insensible . . .
And my face is sad because
Once
There was . . .
Ah, there was a time . . .

Now go look for the mail —
Go glean the thoughts they drop before your door,
You eternal gleaner.
Love thoughts, too . . . ?

> *Out in the hall*
> *The gas jet*
> *Doesn't give a damn that it is day already.*
> *Stench*
> *Of drenched clothes*
> *And snore*
> *Of married men.*
> *Who shall ask the furnished-room poets to write*
> *A song for the dawn?*

Oh, MAIL!
Ah, beggars:

> *"I am-though-I-refrain-from-saying-it better-*
> *than you-in-the-end. I-am-perfectly-honest-*
> *evi-dently-nothing-up-my sleeves . . . It-is-*
> *out-of-my-bounteous-goodness-that-I-like*
> *you-a-little-in spite-of . . ."*

These scanty rights to live —
A clear day, an articulate moment, may take them from us;

So we advance
At every chance
Our suffering claim and reference.

Dragging my soul along
I go to the window.
The sun-fingers reach slowly
Over the face of the house in front.
This is the hour they go to their work
Eastward and westward —
Two processions,
Silent.
Shapeless the hats,
Too large the jackets and shoes —
Grotesques walking,
Grotesques for no one to laugh at.
Are they happy perhaps? —
For, of course . . . but do they
Really know where they're going?
Has the first of them
Found
Down there
Something for his happiness?
And has he telephoned or telegraphed to the others
That they are going,
Without looking around,
Without knowing one another,
ALL
TOGETHER
Eastward and Westward?
The world has decreed:
These men go
Acknowledged
Eastward and Westward.

Sit down and take the rest of your life,
O poets!

All my days
Are in this room
Pressing close against me.
I know what I have done, misdone, mistaken, misunderstood,
*   forgotten, overlooked,*
And I have lost my youth.
Everybody knows me,
No one wonders at me;
They have placed me in their minds, made me small and
*   tied me up*
To throw me in a little dusty corner of their minds.
All my days are huddled
Close against me;
My youth is but a regret and a madness —
A madness . . . Jesus Christ! I am not old yet, never
*   mind what I have told you, what I have been!*
I have not irremediably committed myself, I am not lost —
For pity's sake
Let me go,
Let me go free!
For pity's sake
Let me go
With my youth!

Ah, the old days are huddled
So close against my chest
That no great freeing gesture
Is possible.

After the tears,
Cool, new, sensitive,

Under my body hushed and stiff,
I open the door
Quietly,
I close the door behind me
Carefully.

The street's greeting:
I'm out of work —

Damn work — to work and come home in the evening hungry
            for all the things that could have been done instead!

            But to go
            Unemployed
            Without hunger
            At all!

Oh, listen, O Street,
Let your word to me be a delicate whisper:
I am young,
Nice day,
I look
Straight ahead,
Staccato steps,
Stiff and cool,

I walk
(Sweet morning, soeur de charite!)
It is the light mood in the streets of the morning,
Bouncing on the roofs, kicked
By the rosy foot of the wind.
Ah, we — ah, we are chained to the sidewalk but we hold
            our eyes upward,
Lightly, lightly.
Do blow away the dust of our dead,

And save us all from them who are smouldering inside
      our houses!
See the fine dust from those windows, see the dust angry
      at the sun!
Who threw these kids here among us, them and their fun
      and war, "GIMME! − GIMME!"
King of the triumphing mood, the iceman cracks easy
      puns with a landlady of the dust!
Kaiser of the lightness of the morning, the policeman,
      swinging his stick, writes sacred hieroglyphs.

      Furtively I steal,
      From what and whom
      I know,
      A little youth
      For myself.
      I know nothing,
      I forget nothing,
      I'm glad enough to live
      In the morning.

NOON

You say yes,
And you feed it in your temples — that entity you are so
　　divinely, mysteriously, sure of; and you call it LIFE.
You say no —
In the saloon, the wooden yellow temple,
You grunt no, and you poison that which you call LIFE.
It's noon, the whistles rattle and shriek — city Parcae,
　　I come too.
You say yes
And you grunt NO,
But your faces are faces of rancor:
Rancor against
Those who won't let you
Hurl loose your soul — (you think, you bad philosophers!) —
Which you must steadily
Throttle within you.
Imbecility is an immense maw, and at noon
It is hungry with a thousand crawling hungers.
So that happy bewildered imbecile of a sun
Looks bewildered at me,
Wondering that I am so utterly disgusted.
Not so . . .
Not so disgusted after all.

O altars of a little comfort, altars of a dyspeptic god gone
　　crazy in America for lack of personality (hamburger
　　steak, Irish stew, goulash, spaghetti, chop suey and
　　curry!) O lunch-room counters!
O tripods of a little secure religion, tripods of a little se-
　　cure beauty! O kitchen fires!
O bedraggled romances, O alcoholic ladies in crimson

and green mists, O women so cheap and ingratiate-
ing, O sacrifices for you, ladies, of all the flesh and
all the brains! O saloons!
My malediction on the cowards who are afraid of the
        word *(the word is a kind sweet child, a kind sweet*
        child!) — Malediction on the sacrifices of the dumb
        and deaf!

Hesitating everywhere, hesitating fearfully,
The few poets, they who weigh with delicate hands,
Walk in the unfrequented roads,
Maundering,
Crying and laughing
Against the rest.

AFTERNOON

Over our shoulders
Your noisy anger,
O Elevated!
I walk in a fog of sleep,
Not fearing to be awakened any more.
Something queer to drink,
Or going somewhere else,
Another girl —
These are the last visions of salvation.
The dust has blinded
The trees in the park.
The gutters are loose mouths of the drunken Manhattan
Now at last give them up, your hungry and greasy
And greedy romances.
And you snobs, damn fools, remember you are sweating
          too.
Now at last be all appeased
In ugliness,
Wallow in the heat,
O sacred soul of the crowd.
No one dies, don't be
Afraid.
Some life is left.
See the will-o'-the-wisps of lewdness
Burning in all the eyes.
We are alive yet.

> *See me scuttle on —*
> *Satisfied enough,*
> *Finding with my almost eager eyes*
> *Not-yet-known breasts and strange thighs*
> *In your sacred crowds, O Manhattan!*

EVENING

Tender and young again, feminine, sky of the evening
of summer is blushing.
Round, long and soft like a draped arm, sky of the eve-
ning over the poor city resting.
Spaces of cool blue are musing —
They will hold all our sadness, O spaces of cool blue.
O city, there lived in you once, O Manhattan, a man
WALT WHITMAN.
Our hands are wasted already, perhaps; but enough for
contribution to Beauty.
Enough for a great sadness, will be,
Evening of summer, evening of summer going to sleep
Over the purple bed, over the light flowers of the sunset.
Many other evenings have I in my heart — I have loved so
much, so long and so well — don't you remember
cool blue spaces brooding?
I shall recall you,
I shall recall you if insanity comes and sits down and
puts her hands in my hair.
Once I touched things with religion, once a girl loved me,
once I used to go hiking with young folks over the
Palisades,
Once I cried worthily.

NIGHT

Take me all,
Woman whom I know so well, every wrinkle of you — my
        room---
We won't fight any more.
I have been around, and I have seen the wisdom of you
In the city.
Lay me down over the torn bedspread, let the bed-bugs
        keep me company —
Don't be a prude, old lady:
Your wounds are disgusting enough,
But in the city only the syphilis blooms
And all the other
Flowers are dead.
I will let you reach out with your smell into me.
Literature, eh? —
Blossoms of beggary, morning breath of the sick, dreams
        of the dead!
And I,
Devising sun-spangling images . . . at night, on your
        table! —
With the urge from the soiled-linen box!
Tonight the lie got drunk with sarcasm
And croaked,
Having found nowhere in the city
Self-assertion.
Put me to sleep,
Knock me to sleep:
Or keep me awake and keep a gnaw in my heart working,
If so you please.

Outside a greasy moon
Refuses to understand
How ridiculous her unaesthetic weeping is

If I kill myself . . .
She may . . .
If I kill myself . . .
He may . . .
Would they . . . ?
What would you want, O Death,
Face-of-character,
With a faceless man like me!
Without you, Death,
I am dead.
So I'm going out.
There must be a comfortable little place
For me in the world —
Now I'm dead enough —
I picked it out reading the Evening Journal Sermon
   on Success.
To hell with books — I'll give my young body a chance,
Before my head gets bald.

I will walk with the marionettes
Now I'm dislocated enough and my mouth is clogged.
I'll go talk to them
Now I'm dumb enough.
But come and see me . . .

Oh, do come and see me,
Look down upon me from your place in the sky,
O MY HIGH DREAM!

I have a brain for everything,
I shall dance their ragtime.

Will someone whisper, sometime –
"There is a man who dances
With a strange embarrassment?"

Neuriade

SERMON

Chao-Mong-Mu freely laid his hands over the sky:
You do not know how to lay your hands over the breasts
*   of your beloved.*

Chao-Mong-Mu made the tree dance at his will:
You do not know how to hug a rough tree and say "dar-
*   ling" to it.*

Chao-Mong-Mu magnificently ran a shaft of sunlight
*   to smash against the treetops:*
You walk carefully, carefully, and fend off the sunlight
*   with your grey clothes, although you're very poor.*

Chao-Mong-Mu painted a sky that was a pin-fleshed
*   vase: then he became a very small thing and hid*
*   in the vase:*
You build yourselves immense houses to live in, and you
*   are afraid even there.*

OLD ACCUSTOMED IMPUDEDNT GHOST

That morning the dawn arose from the sodden grey city
   pavements,
And it was a sick grey breath.
I had spent myself asking the night for sleep.

Broken in pieces I was — only the evil spirit was whole
   in me;
There was a curse on my bitten bloody lips . . .
And then . . .

Oh, then the old accustomed, impudent ghost came in:
He wore my bagged, ragged pants, and was unshaven;
And his face was the one I had seen in the mirror
Too many times.

LAKE

Sitting on a bench facing God's beautiful lake,
A poem to God beautiful.

Lake Michigan,
The love a poor sick body held
(Sifted by the sift of a hundred nights of pain),
A poor sick body gave it all to you.

Your absinthe
Has intoxicated me.

Having risen out of your waters,
In front of my great eyes now
There is a mad blur of sunlight,
And the City spread out before me calling from a great
        curve:
"Come, enter, conquistador!"

The line of your horizon, pure and long, hitched to the
        infinite both ways,
Where the mist lies like Peace.
Swimming, I flirted with Death;
Saw death running over the shadow-laced ripples;
And turned around, as you threw water in my eyes,
And laughed at Death, as Death's brother, the devil,
        would.

You slammed open the doors of the sky,
And there stood the tremendous sun.

Lake, gilded in the morning,

I have come out of you,
A fresh-water Neptune;
And the water rang little bells
Trickling down
Along my flesh.
Lake, garden of the colors,
Sweet-breathing mouth of Chicago,
Words die in the fingers of a sick man,
As children dying on a poor father.
Take my promise, lake.

AUBADE

The morning now
Is a white corpse –
The nightmares
Killed her.
Vainly the breeze
Wafts a terrible sadness
Over her body.

ENCOUNTER

Little grey lady sitting by the roadside in the cold,
My fire is to warm you, not to burn you up.

Little grey lady in your little grey house in the warmth,
Your warmth is to loosen my frozen arms and tongue.
Not to drowse me.

INVOCATION TO DEATH

Let me
Close my eyes tight.
Still my arms,
Let me
Be.
Then,
Come!
Let me be utterly alone:
Do not let the awful understanding that comes with
The thought of Death
Bother me.
Your love was not strong enough to hold me.

Death takes things away:
I have them here in my hands,
The rags.

I do not understand the cosmic humor
That lets foolish impossibilities, like me, live.
I have made a mess of it,
But I am no debtor,

It's the yearning of a nervous man,
The yearning for peace,
The curiosity for a word:
Forever.

If She would only come quietly,
Like a lady —
The first lady and the last.

Just not to hear any longer
The noise swelling from the morning streets,
Nor the two desperate sparrows chirruping;
Just not to fear any longer
The landlady.

ITALIAN SONG

Until your lips be red,
Until the winter-time
Until the money be gone,
Until God see us:
Until God see us.

Until old age come, girl,
Until the other man come,
Until the jettatura get me,
Until God see us:
Until God see us.

SMOKE

*All the smoke of the cigarettes of dreamers went over to
the sky, and formed that blue vault you see up there.*

FUNERAL MARCH

The great corpse
Is the crowd.

A whole day
It takes to bury it.

In the morning
They begin;

Not at night,
For they're afraid.

I'm here for . . .
Oh, to wail a great goodbye.

HOPE

Tomorrow will be beautiful,
For tomorrow comes out of the lake.

INSOMNIA

For a year his desperate hands beat the darkness. Then
    out of their rhythm a monster was created:
Three claws on his breast, so that he could not with facil-
    ity heave it;
Three claws on his skull, so that he had waking night-
    mares the year long.
When at last his hands dropped, the monster stooped
    over him, and with his yellow beak plucked out his
    white heart.

SLEEP

At the bottom of the abyss of sleep
A black cradle rocks.
Pain, slight, with evanescent fingers
Pushes it.
Under the cradle is earth,
To cover and stifle you.

TO THE POETS

Essences of the peoples' beautiful selves,
Violins whose strings quiver
With long, soft, delicate harmonies –
Even when touched by the world's rough fingers,
Even when touched by Grief's cold fingers –
Think of the day when you, sleeping in your graves,
Shall be awakened by the thunder of your own voices
And by the strong, cool winds of your own music:
For in the fertile soil of the years
Your voices will blossom and become thunder,
Your music will become winds that purify and create.

WALT WHITMAN

Noon on the mountain! –
And all the crags are husky faces powerful with love for
          the sun;
All the shadows
Whisper of the sun.

WHEN IT HAS PASSED

Love — I thought it was a long ride in a boat
Over a quiet lake: around
The weeping willows let fall their hair
Into the water;
And amid those hairs, the rays
Which the sun had forgotten to take with him going away
Were of indigo-rose-purple-blue.

But now that it has passed I know it was a stream
That swept by roaring, destroying all, all.
In my soul, all that is left is a shrub
That sways and waves at the wind like the hair of a witch.
That whistles and curses the wind like the ghastly arm
            of a witch:
The remembrance.

SENTIMENTAL DIRGE

Sweetheart, what's the use of you –
When the night is blue,
And I'm sad with the whisper of the skies,
And I'm heavy and I'm weary
With my many lies?
There is no music around me –
Not a sound
But the whisper of the skies:
I am bound
To my sadness with so slender, so thin ties –
Oh, so thin, still you can't break them.
Sweetheart, what's the use of you?

And within me, what then pains
When it rains?
Ah, the drops fall on the wound
And it pains.
For my soul's a naked wound,
The rain-drops are salty tears.
Are they tears of some great giant
Who still fears,
Just like me,
For the morrows, for the things that passed away –
For the dead, dead yesterday?
Sweetheart, what's the use of you? –
When the laughters are too few;
When the trees will no more sing
For the wind;
When they wave their ghastly arms,
Naked arms,
In despair, and no one heeds;

And my soul is like the reeds
Stooping under the low wind
Hopelessly — like the reeds,
Broken, that shall rise no more
And sing softly as before —
For the wind has been too cruel
And too strong.

'Neath the snow, wet, lies the fuel:
And the flame
Of my laugher, of all laughters,
Now is dying. Oh, for shame! —
All you promised that first day!
What'll you do for me, now, say,
What'll you do for me?
What's the use
Of you, sweetheart, what's the use?

RUSSIAN BARCAROLLE

Beggars,
Brothers of misery,
Let's pick the silver coin of the moonlight
With
Two heavy, sad
Oars.
       Oh – – – – oh – – –

Chasing
This little beauty,
The cars sweat and cry and dive madly,
Let
Us sink the cars
And-look
       Oh – – –- – oh – – –

And look
For in the moonlight
Our hands are ghastly and tired and shall never
Pick
The moon coin from
The lake.
       the lake – – – the lake – – –

KISS

You think you can leave the matter to your lips
and they don't work right
and then
it's two deadmen shaking hands
saying "Howdydo Sir?"

UTOPIA OF THE MEN WHO COME BACK
FROM THE WAR

I — Listening.

"Ah, my wife,
If we do not chatter,
if we do not wrangle,
we may hear this song —
our love.
Let us just listen,
my wife.

I have learned to be
all hushed,
with a faith,
waiting
when from everywhere
Death was rushing
hurriedly onward."

II — No Return.

For those who live
with their old things
in their old houses:

To go to war
is to go very far from this world,
to go beyond it.

The veterans
never come back.
And the dead also
have gone beyond this old world
forever.

NOCTURNE

The guillotine windowpanes
are both drawn down,
and a curtain nailed to one pane
covers them both and shuts out
(I lie in my bed)
everything but this:

A square of cold
unearthly clean
blue;
In one of the angles
a tiny eighth of moon
gold and silver . . .
and no more . . .

It suffices.

SYNGE'S PLAYBOY OF THE WESTERN WORLD

Variation

It's New York, I tell you . . .
I'd have a home
on top of a hill;
there should be roses
from the roof down;
and I'd get up every day
at sunrise.

I should become so beautiful
you would be embarrassed
looking at me.

It's New York I tell you,
a city that lives
with work
for men stronger than I;
with duties
for a different conscience
than mine.

MORNING SONG

Heavy morning,
With one friend gone
And two loves ended,
Heavy morning.

Heavy morning,
With all the dust
Accumulated
Over these books.

And all the noises
From the street
Unbearable,
Heavy morning,

Heavy morning,
With the ideals
Too long drawn,
With the hopes
Turned stale.

Ah, tired of a miserly
Treachery,
Tired of a cowardly
Subterfuge,
Go to bed again,
Go to bed again.

The street's dissipation
Passes by
Under the window,

With shouts of sad idiots,
The street's dissipation.

Heavy morning,
Be glad
Your eyelids are heavy,
Heavy morning.

Life will go far.
All by herself
To day,
Alone.

SONG

Where has the poppy gone,
at wintertime,
that flaunts again
five blood petals
under the wind's palm?

Between you and me
there is always
a wintertime.
And you are always
like a glowering poppy
when I see you again.

INTERIOR

The lady is a bit of
      Porcelain
Which a rude elbow
Might any minute
      Push
      Down.

The man is a
      Bird of
      Paradise
      Embalmed.

The man is a
      Mouse
      Hungry
      Scurrying
      By.

FOR THREE CHILDREN

DEMAREST LLOYD P., TWO

Altho the radiancy of his big eyes
Be as the sun's glory in the morning,
A shadow of sad secludedness
Watches from them.
He writes for joy,
As he writhes for pain . . .
In the shadow of his eyes looms this destiny:
Great joys and pains will be his –
To be shared with no one –
Bitterly his own.

DENA JULIA P., FOUR

With your blue, almond-cut eyes
You're as sweet as a blue gentian in the grass.
Every motion of you is part of a well-composed dance.
You dance all day long
And it costs nothing to watch you.
They pay Pavlova so much!

CHARLES LESSING P., SEVEN

All of a sudden
You see him stop and be still . . .
His eyes full of sparks and sparkles,
His running-clear-water eyes are still,
Deep and strange . . .
Poor kid
Is he going to be a poet?

A LADY

Her lips are roses
rotting in water

Her eyelids are two shriveled
violets.

Her eyes are puddles.
Her voice is of a bird being strangled.

Her youth in passing
lingers in her hands.
They flutter, hovering
like two butterflies
over the corpse of her flesh.

There is a grim whim in her,
like that of a dead mouth
that smiles.

Her well-rounded legs
tell an impudent lie.

Her soul lies
in the disorder of an orgy
over the ashes and scattered remains of which
hangs, like a thread of blue smoke,
an elegance of tiny gesture.

PORTRAIT, WATER COLOR

In a wood,
With the afternoon sun
Tree-leaves money
And the colors of grass and of violets

A little grey wind
Sneaking away.

The dawn's open-eyed wonder
At the new day

The creaking of old leaves
Under broken, heavy shoes.

In the noontime
From the Earth
To the sky
And from the sky
To the earth.
Up to the blue bowl,
Down into the brown bowl
A shower of petals;
Fragments of sunlight
Are red, green, blue, yellow and orange . . .

How many beautiful women
Are there in the world?

Have you beauty enough
For all the beautiful women of the world?

SERENADE

Come on, don't be afraid you'll spoil me
if you light the gas in your room
and show me
that you have heard my cries.

Are you so poor in kisses
that you're so stingy with them;
and is your heart so ravaged!
that you won't let me pick there
one or two flowers
to stick in my jacket's
button-hole?

I play my serenade
beating with my clenched fist
on a gong and a drum.
What I want is to give you
the sound of what a man is.

I love my eyes and lips
better than yours;
besides, the dampness of the night
pierces my shoes.

I can be as capricious
as you can be, don't worry!

Come on, open that window
or I'll go home.

THE RETURN

To Dorothy Dudley Harvey

I

After eight days of the monotony
Of sea and sky, appeared
City-on-the-rock, proud and beautiful —
Gibraltar.

Then, after two days of Mediterranean,
Monstrous water-lilies of the sea
Budding forth on the ocean —
The Neapolitan islands.

Then the Neapolitan coast,
Besprinkled, as with flowers, with little white houses;
And Mount Vesuvio forgetting its head
In a confusion of cloud and smoke;
Pusilleco, place of trysts.

Here begins my Italy —
Where memories spring like geysers,
Crying at me where I place my feet;
Italy that receives with benignity
This shipwreck — my sick body,
And this feeble candle-light — my soul.

II

I come from America, the land that gathers
The rebels, the miserable, the very poor;

The land of puerile and magnificent deeds;
The naïve skyscrapers — votive candles
At the head of supine Manhattan.

I remember Manhattan Island crowned with docks.

I come from America, where everything
Is bigger, but less majestic;
Where there is no wine.
I arrive in the land of wine —
Wine for the soul.
Italy is a little family;
America is an orphan
Independent and arrogant,
Crazy and sublime,
Without tradition to guide her,
Rushing headlong in a mad run which she calls progress.
Tremendously laborious America,
Builder of the mechanical cities.
But in the hurry people forget to love;
But in the hurry one drops and loses kindness.

And hunger is the patrimony of the emigrant;
Hunger, desolate and squalid —
For the fatherland,
For bread and for women, both dear.
America, you gather the hungry people
And give them new hungers for the old ones.

Where the skyscrapers grow, O America,
You have yelled your name to the four winds;
An ungracious, unkind yell —
That of a sour youth.

You are pitiless for the feeble,
The weak; whereas my country is
A sister of charity.

You are young and hurried; what threatens you,
That you rush so, America?

You are young, and your people,
Pitiless like the young, have hard eyes.
Here eyes are mellowed by the experience
Of two thousand years.
We are old and mellow —
We, the hungry.

How often in the streets of Manhattan
Have I thrown my hatred!
How often in those streets
Have I begged the Universe
To stop that crazy going and coming,
Or to drag me along too in that
Oblivion of hurry.

I have feared for you
The revenge of Love, O America!
How cheap is the sorrow of man!
People eat it with their bread;
It costs little in America —
It doesn't count.

III

Genova with her flights of green trees
On her ascending squares,
Genova that goes to the hills
Like a great staircase.

Modern Bologna, in the late evening,
Seems a bureaucratic bazaar —
With her little shops and the promenading
Of semi-elegant youth.
Old Bologna, with her ancient red palaces
Defying the present. The infinite rows of the porches
Seem the work of an enormous mole.

Remember the lake of Chicago? —
The green absinthe of the lake of Chicago?
How everything has grown small since I went away —
Since I am away!
And how early the city goes to sleep!
Remember Broadway in the night,
Bejeweled?

The Prefettura Palace is like
A squatting hydropical woman.
All offered me a bunch of memories
Fresh and cool like edelweiss.

Bazzano, in a green and brown bowl,
Surrounded by hills as soft to the eyes
As a young woman's breast to the touch;
Bazzano delighted
With the songs of youngsters in the night,
With her church bell eternally in motion,
With her medieval castle on the highest spot of the town,
Challenging the storms that do not come,
Watching.
What and what for do you watch, O Tower?
Austria and the pope have gone their miserable way;
And no danger threatens your fields,
Golden with the white grapes in autumn,

Silver with the new wheat in the spring
Where the snow comes only as a caress.

IV

I have come back, and have found you
All new and friendly, O Fatherland!
I have come back with a great burden,
With the experience of America in my head —
My head which now no longer beats the stars.
O Italy, O great shoe, do not
Kick me away again!

SORROW'S HEADQUARTERS

To Eric Hjorth and Mitchell Dawson.

1 — Sick Men's Hymn

The hospital waits:
I, today, You, tomorrow;
five days, ten days, a month,
six months, a year, ten years;
How much of life have you given the hospital?

Oh, the long hours God steals
from a man's life.
Oh, the dear precious hours
God throws away.

Tumors, broken legs, cancers in the face,
abscesses, bones horribly prominent,
thinness, consumption-sucked faces,
eczema, scabs, eruptions,
Oh, what a funny, happy, gay sculptor and painter
is God?
Yells, roars, jumps and somersaults of epileptics,
Oh, what a happy, gay, funny old Circus Director
is God!

You mock us with your sun
that doesn't warm us,
we, trembling with fever.
With the kind moon we do but see,
we, the blind.
With the green earth our broken legs cannot tread.
With the days and the nights

skipping past us,
(oh, such beautiful dancers)
while we lie helpless and angry.

I talk of you but who are you and who knows you;
You are too distant a promise and we must be dead
in order to see you.
You say you are the light in the midst of our souls,
But I know that in our souls there is only filthy darkness
and the fear of death.

We shall cast over your world our pus and putrefaction:
Let all the flowers be stifled,
what do we care?
The earth is decay to us
and from millions of stinking places
like a monstrous anthem
arises the miasm that is YOU.

You have hidden your promise under the darkness of
           death
You're in bad faith, O, God!
You're no good.

God, give us tonight our rest,
give us tonight our sleep;
Let sleep the sophisticated Lady, embrace us.
Let sleep come, slay her thousand
little enemies.
Let our filthy thirsty wounds be quenched,
Let pain knock at our head
a tremendous lullaby.

2 — The Doctor

Very elegant
in spite of age
finds enough warmth
in his heart
to embrace woman
and whisper
in her ears
shocking and thrilling
little mysteries of love.

His wife's death
veiled his face,
but that was
for a while:
now, his sarcastic but large laugh
is victorious again.

He is erect
like Apollo Senior.

His voice is
a kind obstinacy.
His smile is
a little muddled.
His life is
a dance of operations.
With his nickel-plated instruments
hidden under his coat,
he dances over Bazzano.
He skips and flutters
over Bazzano,
knowing that sickness
is a whim of God.

3 — The Catholic Sisters

The sisters seem large butterflies.
In the darkness of corridors
they stir,
like a lugubrious promise.

Their faces show their barrenness:
Green apples left to rot on the ground.
Green apples with the worm
of satiated chastity in them.
>*I told Sister Claire: You say your God is just:*
>*Why then the torture of infants and of the just.*
>"Because of the original sin" *she said.*

>*I told Sister Claire:*
>*Why was Adam put into the world when God knew*
>*beforehand that he was going to sin.* "That is
>a matter of philosophy. Ask our priest!" *Thus*
>*Sister Claire.*

>*I told Sister Joan: I love you.* "If it's true I'll
>tell the mother superior." *No, it isn't true, I*
>*said.*

4 — Morphine

I stared into a near world
Populated with mutilated images.

The clouds of a tempestuous rage
subdued, sail slowly toward me.

And in these clouds scattered
disorderly,
the gnomes of sleepiness
play a dreary comedy.

Arms dangled and were loosened
from their sockets
and the legs had a will of their own.

With the scintillating sword of my open eyes
I opened me a way among the gnomes of sleepiness
that attacked my head — an undefended fortress.

There was a wavering, a hesitation,
and then the gnomes sailed away to the infinite
over a shaft of sunlight.

They came back, having brought
news of me to the infinite,
and I was rocked again to desultory sleep.

5 — A Warning from Age

Through my hair
the comb passes
quickly, quickly.

6 — Song

Let me look for my heart:
Is it perhaps on the top of an apple tree, the apples of
     which I used to steal as a child, that I shall find it?

Let me find my heart:
Is it perhaps on the rocks of the Ponente Riviera
    in a dark blue hole,
together with a tiny octopus, that I shall find it?
Let me look for my heart:
Is it perhaps at the foot of a skyscraper, trampled upon
    by a million people, that I shall find it?

Let me find my heart:
Is it perhaps in the bosom of my beloved, that I shall
    find it?
Cut open that breast pitilessly and let us see!

Let me look for my heart:
Is it perhaps squeezed between two pages of a book that
    I shall find it?
What a miserable state it must be in!

Let me find my heart:
My heart has lost itself in clouds that resemble princesses
    on horseback. The breezes of the upper skies cool
    it and they carry on their backs sweet names for it.

7 — In Grey

The day weighs upon me like a ton of smoke.
Things already done are
cadavers filling with stench
the grey rooms of my memories.
The future is a series of
still-born children.

The pool of oblivion is muddy.
Only slow-marching memories

come along the road of today. Grey sky
to awaken me momentarily.

But dismal sleep is today's program:
sleep that rises out of the heart
like black gas.

I know
that for having slept much
the dead have grown strong.
On days as these
they kick open their graves
and skip elegantly out.
They whisper horrible secrets
to each other and to me.
They carry their shrouds and
shake them valiantly.

O Goddess of dismay and melancholy
come to my help!
I still have withered kisses for you,
kisses I don't want to throw away for I'm very poor,
cleave me away from my memories.

They bother me so that sleep flirts and flees,
flirts and flees.

8 — The talkative Poet follows a Catholic Procession

De Profundis clamavi ad Te Domine
Out of an inscrutably deep grotto
Comes a white body.

He speaks: "I have lived under the sea
The tremor of the surf reached my supine body."

Domine exaudi vocem meam.
weeping willows murmuring in the sunset fragrance
"We, the sorrowing friends of the trees
pay with our tears the toll.
The passing water is hurried,
but can't forget to kiss
our hair.
We murmur tonight for Grace is near
for the trees our friend and for our bending heads."

Si iniquitates observaveris, Domine, Domine quis sus-
tinebit.

Sodom is burning.
Over its jagged profile
a crown of flame is set.
By the thin hand of Fate
a baby is held
over the city.
Tomorrow in the ashes and cinders they shall find it.
And they shall carry it away
to the land of silver rivers.

Quia apud Te propitiatio est; et propter legem tuam
sustinui Te Domine.
Diplomats and lawyers are at a dinner:
Theft, raping, white slavery etc., etc.
these are the fruits upon their tables.
They poison themselves with gusto and throw away the
core of the fruits.
They throw it in the nearby fields
of journalism, for the journalists to eat.

Et ipse redimet Israel ex omnibus iniquitatibus ejus.
Israel's redemption is accomplished.
And the iniquities are scattered about
Like small toads on a humid summer night.

Et lux perpetua luceat eis.
Evergreens cool the hot scene of a heaven aflame.

9 — Dolce Cuore

(When you say "Dolce" to him he answers "Cuore"
which two words are the beginning of an ejaculation
thus: "Dolce Cuor del mio Gesu, fa ch'io t'ami sempre
piu" "Sweet heart of my Jesus, make me love you ever
more!")

This slimy old man
this mass of irresponsible flesh,
this ridiculous warrior against old age,
this man is religious.

He is religious like a bug
that contemplates the ocean
and thinks of crossing it;
like a dog lapping up milk from a bowl
of untouched gold;
like a dirty-winged butterfly;
like lace used for cleaning machinery;
like a bear picking daisies,
like slime on a silver spoon.

He tries to live a saint's life:
eating rubbish and sleeping on the ground

eating even dog.
This latest day saint.

When he came to the hospital he said:
"Me go under those clean sheets and soil them?
Nothing doing!"
The candor of lingerie dazzled him
This big toad bewildered by sudden light.

He ate with such avidity that he was struck
by a tremendous colic,
with a forty fever and the certainty that he would die.
He wanted then to leave Bazzano immediately
to have his bones at rest over his native mountain.
Or was it native dunghill?

He cannot stand even the presence of a certain nurse
that exasperates him spanking him
and lifting the curtains that cover his shames
in front of strangers.
This horribly chaste Diana.
He is always in anxiety for fear of losing the
esteem of the sisters.
This little boy blue of eighty.

His life has been a pilgrimage:
He went twenty times to Loretto
and to Rome where he almost spoke with the pope.
He stinks of sanctity.
He passes his life
between caring for his chickens and going to mass.
This careful housewife.

In the summer he rents his house to gentlemen
but his sister must come and rake up his house

a little.
He, then, lives the life of a bird in the woods.
This slimy little bird.

Once a nurse dropped two pieces of bread
he had found on the night-table into the pot
and he picked up the bread exclaiming:
"Rather burst than waste!"
This illustrious economist.

Oh, dolce, dolce!
"Cuore, Cuore!"

Afterword

"A Man Must Yell If He Wants To Be Heard"

Dennis Barone

*E*manuel Carnevali (born Florence 1898, died Bazzano 1941/42) remains an almost mythological figure. Anyone who knows anything about poetry written in English between the two World Wars knows the name Carnevali, but almost no one knows the words of the wonderful work he wrote. Most of those who did know it and who praised its author or supported him after illness forced his return to Italy where he suffered for years in a spartan hospital room, have long since died. Edward Dahlberg, for example, recalled a pilgrimage he made: "I was so enthralled by *A Hurried Man* [the one book Carnevali published during his lifetime] that I went to Bazzano, a hilly medieval town, two and a half hours by steam train from Bologna, to visit" Carnevali (55). His one book that Robert McAlmon and William Bird published in 1925 all but disappeared. His dear friend Kay Boyle prepared a second work of Carnevali's several decades after his death, a book that includes some of the prose contents of the first one and two of the poems. Furthermore, Carnevali's poems appear squeezed into his 1925 book. Prose sections of autobiographically based fiction, memoir, literary essays, and reviews precede and follow the poems and by these weighty bookends some of the power of these poems and their capability to stand alone as a beautiful and complete book-as-poem becomes diminished.

Upon his first appearance in *Poetry* (March 1918), six poems following "A Dance-play for Poem-mimes" by Alfred Kreymborg, the editors described Carnevali as a young poet "who was born in Florence twenty years ago, was educated in Italian technical schools, and came to America at sixteen. Since then he has earned his living in various difficult ways, studied English, and written his first poems [...]" (343). This is a remarkable immigrant story, but there's so much more to it. By February 1931, Carnevali's last appearance in the magazine, his contributor's note stated simply that he is the author of *A Hurried Man* and lives in Bazzano, Italy as if the biography of this man now slowed by encephalitis had so many twists and turns that it needed deadpan understatement to straighten it out. Lives in Bazzano! What kind of life did he live? His mother died when he was ten. He went to the home of his despised father, spent some years in a number of schools, and then ran away to America where he worked, when he could get work, most often as a waiter. But for a brief period of six months in 1919 he served as Associate Editor of *Poetry* in Chicago and abandoned in New York his young wife, Emily, who he had married the year before when he was a mere nineteen. (Ellen Williams in her history of *Poetry* briefly mentions Carnevali on pages 260 and 265. That's it!) He became physically ill while in Chicago and then also had a mental breakdown. After hospitalization he wandered the shores of Lake Michigan. (Sherwood Anderson, one of Carnevali's Chicago friends, wrote in his *Memoirs* that at this time he "lost all track" of Carnevali. "What was his final end," he said, "I never knew" [404].) Other friends underwrote his return to Italy and there, for the most part, he spent the remainder of his life drugged or shaking or shaking and drugged in a hospital room. Boyle wrote in the "Afterword" to the memoir *Being Geniuses Together* that in 1941 Carnevali, this poet who so wanted to write, "died in Bazzano of what is known as 'the silent death.' Long after the war was over," she explained, "we learned that, abandoned and alone, he had choked on a piece of bread caught in his windpipe" (340). Yet, his date of death is usually listed as 1942.

William Carlos Williams devoted four pages of his *Autobiography* (266-269) to Carnevali. Sherwood Anderson dedicated a poem, "A Dying Poet," to him. In his essay for the Objectivist issue of *Poetry* (February 1931) in which Carnevali had a translation of a Rimbaud poem, Louis Zukofsky quoted Ezra Pound on Carnevali: "'For a number of years one has recognized that Carnevali was one of the few who *might*, and one has speculated as to whether his handicap was too great. It seems to me that the time has now come when one can without reservation recognize his validity as a writer'" (269). And that *is* high praise from Pound. Despite all this his work remains unread today. During his lifetime, as Mario Domenichelli has written, "Carnevali always kept on the treshold, never really belonging to anywhere, a guest everywhere, a stranger, a perpetual outsider" (84).

Kay Boyle noted in her "Preface" to Carnevali's writings, his *Autobiography* that she partly compiled:

> Sometimes it would take Carnevali a day to do a sentence, a week to do a paragraph, for while he shook with the terrible ague of illness, he would have to hold his right hand in the grip of his left in order to be able to strike the keys. (15)

Yet from the hospital in Bazzano – "this palace of pus and blood, in the bedlam of the cries of the ill, nailed to a bed I scarcely ever left" (*Autobiography* 202), he managed to eke out poems, stories, and an extensive correspondence. This is remarkable, but no more so than the fact that in *Poetry* magazine alone he published thirty-nine poems, twenty-six reviews, and six essays from his first appearance in 1918 until his last in 1931.

Among the reasons for struggling to maintain through correspondence his connection to the outside world were to thank those who aided him financially and to solicit response to his writing. In 1927 Boyle succeeded in obtaining a small monthly donation for Carnevali from the affluent contemporary poet Blanche Matthias. Boyle wrote:

> I wonder if you could do something for Emanuel Carnevali. He is ill and in need as you know, and even five dollars a month is a fortune to him. If you could send him that amount it would be a Godsend to him.

Matthias became one of Carnevali's "five-dollar friends," as he put it in one letter to her. In every letter he wrote to her he thanked her for the money and sometimes added a reminder to send next month's check, but much more emphatically he asked for response to his writing. "I am a writer and I write about persons and things," he straightforwardly declared near the beginning of *A Hurried Man* (20). And so immediately after thanking Matthias in one letter he wrote, "The next time I hear from you I'd want you to talk to me about my book and how you liked it and how you didn't. [...] It is my warm and happy son, it is my bones and my flesh, it is my heart and my liver." He wrote in one essay, "I was frantically in need of praise, crazy about my being considered a major poet. The fact that there may be other poets better than I makes my heart sick" (*Autobiography* 93).

He would also tell correspondents about his health. In one letter to Matthias he wished his benefactor good health "for a poet should be healthy. So that the bushwah may not say that poetry is a weakness" and in another he told her, "I am a miserable man, Blanche Matthias, I belong to the dead and if it weren't for my work which I really love I should have probably ended it all."

Occasionally, Carnevali asked others for something more specific than money or praise. Carnevali asked Ezra Pound for a warm hat and some neckties. Pound sent books, magazines, money, an overcoat, three shirts, and assorted neckties, but apparently Pound never sent a hat. Yet, Carnevali was immensely thankful for Pound's aid. He questioned Pound about his fascist sympathies and also wrote, "You are my best almost my only friend." Near the end of Carnevali's life Pound forsook him: perhaps, because of strong differences in political beliefs?

Carnevali had a conflictual relationship with so many things: Modernism, America, and Italy among them. While some readers and scholars associate immigrant writing with an anti-Modernist literary realism, not all early Italian American writing used a realist narrative style or opposed Modernist developments. Guiseppe Cautela, for example, composed his 1925 novel *Moon Harvest* in a poetic expressionistic prose. Carnevali steeped himself in international experimental Modernism. Yet, in his *Autobiography*, he recorded that he told the authors associated with the avant-garde magazine *Others*, "you are irremediably, tremendously different from what I am" (142). On the other hand, in his biographical note for his first contribution to *Poetry* he claimed to have rejected Italian literature and to have embraced a number of American authors. Of Italian Futurism he wrote: "The movement, being largely a furious reaction, was largely a merely negative manifestation. [...] Above all, let's hate the bourgeois. The trouble with them [the Futurists] was [...] that they were bourgeois themselves" (*Autobiography* 127). Elsewhere in the *Autobiography* he wrote, "I felt I belonged to the nineteenth century more than to any other, perhaps entirely, insanely to the nineteenth century" (176).

However, much like his friend William Carlos Williams who in his 1918 "Prologue" to *Kora in Hell* said "our prize poems are especially to be damned not because of superficial bad workmanship, but because they are rehash, repetition" (24), Carnevali believed that the poet must write in a language commensurate with his times. As he put it in his essay "Dante – And Today":

> We are waiting for the poet who will give us a *Divina Commedia* of our own times, but it is something entirely different from Dante's that we expect. A hell more terrific than the hell of Dante is the hell of modern warfare – an immense, eyeless stupid machine that batters, mangles, crushes, distorts, tortures, crazes men. (*A Hurried Man* 185)

He referred to the world in which he lived – in literary modernist vein – as a "tremendous factory": "Out of this factory the human soul comes crushed – out of this factory of neurosis, the modern world. Machines and neurosis, out of this factory!" (*A Hurried Man* 186). The poet he recommended for the times: Carl Sandburg. Of Bodenheim, Kreymborg, Ridge, and Williams he proclaimed on one occasion: "You are the drunken Earth of the transition 1890-1915. The Earth has proceeded and left you behind in the black emptiness" (*A Hurried Man* 265). Sandburg, however, according to Carnevali, wrote in "a purely [...] American language [...] and a language of today" (*A Hurried Man* 233). Yet, if it is a response to a modern hell that Carnevali sought in his poetic ideal, then Sandburg who finds, according to Carnevali, "in the smoke and the dirt [...] youth, human tenderness and hope," seems an odd choice.

McAlmon claimed that Carnevali's "critical articles and short stories in those days were about the best" (*Being Geniuses Together* 136). Yet he found Carnevali's love for certain American authors misguided. "I concluded that it was because he was a foreigner that he so passionately loved Whitman, and later Sherwood Anderson and Carl Sandburg. Neither Anderson nor Sandburg rang true to me" (136). But remember Carnevali wrote with a youthful energy and enthusiasm and he would often contradict himself or change his mind. Pound, for example, became a close friend, but in one of his early strongly stated essays Carnevali wrote that the word one associates with Ezra Pound "is Irritation. Irritation inspires him and he inspires irritation in his readers" (*A Hurried Man* 189-190). Later in this review essay he said of Pound's writing: "a sulking, aggressive, self-conscious man scowls at you from behind every sentence" (191).

Some years later when Carnevali and Pound became friends the former once wrote to the latter that he envied Pound's ability to write so prolifically. He told Pound it makes him "crazy" that he can't write so much as a single story without spending the rest of his life fretting about it. (Curiously, he seems here to blame a weakness in spirit or will rather than ill health for what he regarded as a meager literary output.) Carnevali worried about being a one-book author and that one book, as Williams put it, "no one remembers" despite it being, as Williams said in his *Autobiography*, "one of the best examples of – what? a book, a book that is all of a man, a young man, superbly alive. Doomed" (276). McAlmon, the primary publisher of *A Hurried Man* (the book bears the imprint of both Contact Editions and William Bird's Three Mountains Press) and the person who compiled Carnevali's writings into that order, that book; stated in *Being Geniuses Together* that such books had little distribution and since "the books were printed in English on the Continent" they became "suspect by both the English and the American customs officers" (91). In particular, "one shipment of *A Hurried Man* [...]

was rejected and never returned" (91). Since McAlmon and Bird printed editions of three hundred to five hundred copies, confiscated shipments meant disaster. If the books did reach America, McAlmon said, "they were referred to as Paris and expatriate productions even if their authors were living, and had been living, in America" (304).

Although Boyle succeeded in finding a publisher for Carnevali's *Autobiography* in 1967, Carnevali himself had tried to obtain some interest in it as early as 1930/31. In a letter to Richard Johns, editor of *Pagany*, he noted, "I have received the Fall number of *Pagany* but haven't heard from you whether you like or don't my autobiography." In a letter to Williams, Carnevali asked his friend to encourage Johns to publish this second book in installments. "Above all," Carnevali stated late in the *Autobiography* as finally published long after his death, "I was an envious man, madly jealous of all the writers who had got out more than one book" and he admitted that as far as publishing more than a single work he "was like a dog barking at stones which he cannot pick up and throw" (194). Part of his autobiography in process did appear in the 1932 anthology *Americans Abroad*.

But isn't it remarkable, nonetheless, that a maligned immigrant soul later racked with physical discomfort and pain accomplished so much? A life-story is never simple and even after death it cannot be reduced to mere formula: he was this and he was that – the eulogy will not suffice. Carnevali left Italy, a country "from whom" he "received" very little (*Autobiography* 61), but when he happened "to sing an Italian song in the streets" of America, he "started to weep like a fool" (62). The protagonist of John Fante's *1933 Was a Bad Year*, Dominic Molise, says of his grandparents' world, "There had been poverty in Abruzzi too, but it was a sweeter poverty that everyone shared like bread passed around" (18). At times, this is the way Carnevali felt in America.

Then, too, he felt a general disappointment in the architecture and cityscape of New York. Venice, for Carnevali, had been all white lace, but New York "was one of the great disillusions of [his] entire unhappy life" (*Autobiography* 73). He described it as an "awful network of fire-escapes" and a "miserable panorama" (73). It "was no great city but a great village. It lacked the air, the smell, the noise, the atmosphere of a metropolis" (74). When Jean-Paul Sartre toured the United States in 1945, he observed that originally every American city was "a camp in the desert" (114). Whereas Sartre traveled in ease and comfort, Carnevali struggled to survive.

As soon as he arrived in New York, he wrote, he began his "life in the rooming-house, the furnished rooms of America" (*Autobiography* 74). Parenthetically, he wrote, some one-dozen pages later:

> How much of myself have I left in furnished rooms, such as my falling hair which I left on every pillow? How much of my life has been torn and lacerated and abused and enslaved by the furnished rooms of America? If all the hours I spent in furnished rooms could be strung as beads are strung they would form the notes of one eternal howl that might perhaps at last reach the ears of God. (87)

Yet, his situation, he believed was typical, not unique: "the furnished room welcomes with miserable arms the hopeless rebels of the earth. I am the typical American, – see? [...] The true American home is the furnished-room" (*A Hurried Man* 53-54). But, nonetheless, he could also say, "New York, my city" (*A Hurried Man* 248).

It was during his time in New York that he met "the dearest friend of [his] life": Louis Grudin. Grudin introduced Carnevali to many American writers and like the friendship between Pietro di Donato and Louis Ducoff, Carnevali felt "curiously satisfied" with his close relationship with an urban Jewish intellectual (*Autobiography* 101). Such friendships enabled the laboring Italian immigrant (or son of immigrants) to receive encouragement for the accomplishments of the mind. Grudin probably influenced his friend's position on Modernism. In an essay that serves as the preface for a 1934 collection of his poems, Grudin wrote: "The rapid succession of short-lived critical faiths in the past twenty years was a series of attempts to solve the dilemmas of the literary artist under the stress of catastrophic social changes as they altered his life and the conditions and materials of his art" (xiii) and in "Job Junior," the essay by Carnevali that serves as the preface to the present volume, we read: "All the old truths are true today, too, but the world has gone ahead without hearing them. [...] Today wants new approaches, new absurdities, new crazes, new dances, new dislocations. Today does not want truth." Grudin wrote: "The seer, the *priestly* artist, is now a neurotic and a fraud, a creature of processes beyond his control and he is in the same state of subjection no matter what armed camp captures his loyalty" (xvi). And Carnevali from his essay on the *Others* group: "I am disgusted with your little-review talk of technique and technicians" (*A Hurried Man* 264). No matter who influenced whom, they learned much from each other. "We walked sometimes the whole night through," Carnevali recalled, "shouting our ideas to the stars and the moon, awfully glad we were intelligent [...]" (*Autobiography* 101).

For a brief time Carnevali tried to deny his own ethnicity: "I passed for a Frenchman, because I had come to the conclusion that Italians were not well seen out of Italy" (*Autobiography* 88). Fante's protagonist in "The Odyssey of a Wop," his most well known story, asks, "Doesn't my name sound French? Sure! So thereafter, when people ask me my nationality, I tell them I am French" (136).

Carnevali worked in New York, when he could find work, as a dishwasher or waiter. "'Work! Sure! For America beautiful will eat you and spit your bones into the earth's hole! Work!'" So declares one of the Italian immigrant construction workers on the opening page of Pietro di Donato's novel *Christ in Concrete* (3). Carnevali felt much the same. "The days I was not employed by work I was employed by hunger," he said (*Autobiography* 84) and added, "America, great workhouse of the strong, you almost crushed me, but now and then I was able to rise to the surface and fight back." Much like another Italian American immigrant writer of the 1920s, Pascal D'Angelo, literary aspirations at times kept him going; at others, those aspirations almost drove him mad. D'Angelo, too, achieved some fame in the 1920s, but there is a crucial difference in how the two men reacted to their success: D'Angelo refused to forsake his fellow workers whereas Carnevali typified the avant-garde egoist and would do what he deemed best to fulfill his ambition, family and friends be damned.

D'Angelo's mentor, Carl Van Doren, said that D'Angelo's "fame might have enabled its possessor to accept any one of several editorial positions," but he didn't do so, according to Van Doren, because he had "artistic tact," in other words editing is something of less worth than writing (xi). But that was not the reason to decline offers. As D'Angelo put it in the final pages of his autobiography, "I am not deserting the legions of toil to refuge myself in the literary world. No! No! I only want to express the wrath of their mistreatment. No! I seek no refuge! I am a worker, a pick and shovel man" (165).

Carnevali, on the other hand, was ego-focused and felt little solidarity with the dishwashers and waiters of the world and competitive closeness with the writers of the world. "The first good poem that was ever written started the school of Homer, Dante and Shakespeare; and in so far as a poet succeeds in writing poetry, he belongs to that school and no other" (*A Hurried Man* 220-21). Carnevali did accept his first opportunity for editorial work. Harriet Monroe of *Poetry* arranged for the boy-genius to move to Chicago and to assist an Italian Protestant minister with the publication of a journal. He was soon fired and then he went to work at *Poetry*, but there, too, he noted, "I was an undesirable worker and Harriet Monroe was dissatisfied with me. I must admit that I deserved her reproaches for I was a lazy good-for-nothing sort of cub" (*Autobiography* 157). Harriet Monroe wrote that, "It would take a novel [...] to deal with the rebellious spirit and hapless life of Emanuel Carnevali" (420). In her memoir she recalled that, "He would slam into the office at chance moments, dash through a few manuscripts with violent contempt, skip all dull routine work, and dash out again for more romantic explorations" (422). Although she felt "unspeakable relief" when "he left Chicago [...] and sailed from New York for Italy," she also expressed some regret. "The literary career which had begun brilliantly with memorable stories and poems, the genius which had been prophetically acclaimed by various critics, could not go on to a triumph" (422).

The poems published here – the poems originally included in *A Hurried Man* – are a triumph. They are a Song of Carnevali, an immigrant's hymn, and a dying man's lament. These "monstrous anthems" contain all that is in both *A Hurried Man* and the *Autobiography*. What I mean by this is that the poems take us from New York to Chicago and his illness and then to his return to Italy and those painful years in a hospital room. These poems can stand alone as a book-as-a-poem, one continuous long-poem narrative, in a sense. But in every sense, they are today as they were before this day and will be again tomorrow "one of the best examples of – what? a book, a book that is all of a man, a young man, superbly alive. Doomed" (Williams, *Autobiography* 267).

Carnevali's essay "Job Junior" has been included here as a preface to his work; it provides an understanding of his poetics. McAlmon included this essay in *A Hurried Man* (61-79). It originally appeared in *Youth, a magazine of the arts* (January, 1922). I have made a few changes in spelling and punctuation in both the essay and the poems. Carnevali once wrote in a letter to Pound that he appreciated Louis Zukofsky's changes in his Rimbaud translation included in the Objectivist issue of *Poetry* magazine. He told Pound: "Thank him for it, will you?" May my small choices, my minor "retouching" also be so worthy. Leonardo Buonomo has said that Carnevali "flashed like a meteor across the scene of modern American literature" (187). May this book allow Carnevali's flame to shine once more and may his literary star ascend to its much-deserved height.

Emanuel Carnevali should have the last word. He told Pound that he thought "Italian Farmer" his best poem. Richard Johns published it in *Pagany* (Fall 1930), and here it is:

ITALIAN FARMER

Years of bending to his spade
have cast a weight upon him, so that he is
hunchback.
The patches of his pants (for hardly ever does he wear a jacket)
form the most ridiculous and yet the most tragic
flag. His shirt
is unspeakably dirty.

The earth, that damn stepmother,
has sucked his flesh
so that he is a mass of contracted muscles.

His gnarled face, where no human feelings can be discerned,
is a mask of many sorrows, much pain and no vanity at all.
The sun and the moon he never knew or saw
for he never lifted his face to the sky.
Sky is merely the recipient of rain for him,
sky is the place where an improbable God sits doing nothing;
stars are things that make little light;
the sun is what scorches him in the summer and what makes
little heat in the winter.
He bends down to the earth and asks for nothing:
knowing too well the earth is a traitor which gives and does not
give. His songs are unbeautiful, for songs mean laziness
and this farmer would die if he didn't work.
Wine cannot kill him or give him peace.
His drunkenness is as black as his soberness.
Drunkenness of no laughter, dark, drunkenness of damnation.
Drunkenness that is near to death.
Silent he is but no sphinx,
his sorrow is plain enough; in fact
it is often paltry too.
When he is drunk he sings songs that have
the sadness of an ass braying.
He has no great sorrow because his soul is small,
but he resents the darkness of his soul, for that
eats at his heart like the philoxera that eats
the roots of the grape trees.
What if his fields are beautiful in the sun,
what if his grapes weigh sometimes five kilo to a bunch,
he thinks only what he has to gain by all of them,
and a veil of ugliness descends at once over them all for his eyes to see.
He knows the rage of seeing that the earth does not respond to his care.
He knows the despair after a thunderstorm that brings with it the terrible
                                        all-destroying hail.

Hardly ever is he religious,
considering, not wrongly I think, that religion
is a thing for women and children.
Love is too delicate an affair for him,
and women are damnable and useless.

Anderson, Sherwood. *Sherwood Anderson's Memoirs: A Critical Edition*. Ed. Ray Lewis White. Chapel Hill: U of North Carolina P, 1969.

———. "To A Dying Poet." *A New Testament*. New York: Boni and Liveright, 1927. 98-100.

Boyle, Kay. "Letter to Blanche Matthias." 19 July 1927. Blanche Matthias Papers. The Beinecke Rare Book & Manuscript Library, Yale University, New Haven, CT.

———. "Preface." *The Autobiography of Emanuel Carnevali*. New York: Horizon P, 1967. 9-19.

Buonomo, Leonardo. "A 'Lost Soul' in America: Emanuel Carnevali's Autobiography." *Remembering the Individual / Regional / National Past*. Ed. Waldemar Zacharasiewicz. Tubingen: Stauffenberg Verlag, 1999. 187-96.

Carnevali, Emanuel. *The Autobiography of Emanuel Carnevali*. Ed. Kay Boyle. New York: Horizon P, 1967.

———. "The First God." *Americans Abroad*. Ed. Peter Neagoe. The Hague: The Servire P, 1932. 73-82.

———. *A Hurried Man*. Paris: Contact Editions, Three Mountains P, 1925.

———. "Italian Farmer." *Pagany* 1.4 (1930): 52-53.

———. "Letters to Blanche Matthias." No date. Blanche Matthias Papers.

———. "Letters to Ezra Pound. 1930-1937." Ezra Pound Papers. The Beinecke Rare Book & Manuscript Library, Yale University, New Haven, CT.

———. "Letters to Richard Johns." No date. *Pagany* Papers. Special Collections, Morris Library, University of Delaware, Newark, DE.

———. "Letter to William Carlos Williams." No date. *Pagany* Papers.

Cautela, Guiseppe. *Moon Harvest*. New York: Dial P, 1925.

Dahlberg, Edward. "The Expatriates: A Memoir." *Alms for Oblivion*. Minneapolis: U of Minnesota P, 1964. 51-59.

D'Angelo, Pascal. *Son of Italy*. 1924. Toronto: Guernica Editions, 2003.

Di Donato, Pietro. *Christ in Concrete*. 1939. New York: Penguin, 1993.

Domenichelli, Mario. "Emanuel Carnevali's 'great good bye.'" *Beyond the Margins: Readings in Italian Americana.* Ed. Paolo A. Giordano and Anthony Julian Tamburri. Madison, NJ: FDU P, 1998. 83-94.

Fante, John. *1933 Was a Bad Year.* Santa Rosa, CA: Black Sparrow P, 1985.

———. "The Odyssey of a Wop." 1940. *The Wine of Youth: Selected Stories.* Santa Rosa, CA: Black Sparrow P, 1985. 133-146.

Grudin, Louis. "Preface: Poetry and Causal Symbolism." *A Tearless Glass: With a Preface on the Art of Poetry.* New York: Covici Friede Publishers, 1934. i-xxiv.

McAlmon, Robert, and Kay Boyle. *Being Geniuses Together: 1920-1930.* San Francisco: North Point P, 1984.

Monroe, Harriet. *A Poet's Life: Seventy Years in a Changing World.* New York: Macmillan, 1938.

Poetry. March 1918.

Poetry. February 1931.

Sartre, Jean-Paul. "American Cities." *Literary and Philosophical Essays.* New York: Collier Books, 1962. 114-25.

Van Doren, Carl. "Introduction." *Son of Italy*, by Pascal D'Angelo. New York: Macmillan, 1924. ix-xiii.

Williams, Ellen. *Harriet Monroe and the Poetry Renaissance: The First Ten Years of POETRY, 1912-22.* Urbana: U of Illinois P, 1977.

Williams, William Carlos. *The Autobiography of William Carlos Williams.* 1951. New York: New Directions, 1967.

———. "Prologue." *Kora in Hell: Improvisations.* 1920. *Imaginations.* New York: New Directions, 1970. 6-28.

About the Editor

Dennis Barone is Professor of English and Chair of the English Department at Saint Joseph College in West Hartford, Connecticut. He is the author of three books of short fiction: *Abusing the Telephone* (Drogue Press, 1994), *The Returns* (Sun & Moon Press, 1996), and *Echoes* (Potes & Poets Press, 1997). *Echoes* received the 1997 America Award for most outstanding book of fiction by a living American writer. He is also the author of two novellas, *Temple of the Rat* (Left Hand Books, 2000) and *God's Whisper* (Spuyten Duyvil, 2005). *Precise Machine*, a hybrid work of memoir, prose poetry, and short fiction, has been published recently by Quale Press. He is editor of *Beyond the Red Notebook: Essays on Paul Auster* (University of Pennsylvania Press, 1995), and author of the collection of short prose pieces, *The Walls of Circumstance* (Avec Books, 2004). Left Hand Books published his selected poems, entitled *Separate Objects*, in 1998. His essays on American literature and culture have appeared in journals such as *American Studies, Critique, Proceedings of the American Philosophical Society, Review of Contemporary Fiction,* and *Voices in Italian Americana.* A graduate of Bard College, he received his PhD in American Civilization from the University of Pennsylvania in 1984, and in 1992 he held the Thomas Jefferson Chair, a distinguished Fulbright lecturing award, in the Netherlands.

EMANUEL DI PASQUALE
The Silver Lake Love Poems
Vol. 21, Poetry, $7.00

JOSEPH TUSIANI
Ethnicity
Vol. 20, Selected Poetry, $12.00

JENNIFER LAGIER
Second Class Citizen
Vol. 19, Poetry, $8.00

FELIX STEFANILE
The Country of Absence
Vol. 18, Poetry, $9.00

PHILIP CANNISTRARO
Blackshirts
Vol. 17, History, $12.00

LUIGI RUSTICHELLI, ED.
Seminario sul racconto
Vol. 16, Narrativa, $10.00

LEWIS TURCO
Shaking the Family Tree
Vol. 15, Poetry, $9.00

LUIGI RUSTICHELLI, ED.
Seminario sulla drammaturgia
Vol. 14, Theater/Essays, $10.00

Fred L. Gardaphè
Moustache Pete is Dead!
Long Live Moustache Pete!
Vol. 13, Oral literature, $10.00

JONE GAILLARD CORSI
Il libretto d'autore, 1860–1930
Vol. 12, Criticism, $17.00

HELEN BAROLINI
Chiaroscuro: Essays of Identity
Vol. 11, Essays, $15.00

T. PICARAZZI AND W. FEINSTEIN, EDS.
An African Harlequin in Milan
Vol. 10, Theater/Essays, $15.00

JOSEPH RICAPITO
Florentine Streets and Other Poems
Vol. 9, Poetry, $9.00

FRED MISURELLA
Short Time
Vol. 8, Novella, $7.00

NED CONDINI
Quartettsatz
Vol. 7, Poetry, $7.00

ANTHONY JULIAN TAMBURRI, ED.
MARY JO BONA, INTROD.
Fuori: Essays by Italian/American
Lesbians and Gays
Vol. 6, Essays, $10.00

ANTONIO GRAMSCI
PASQUALE VERDICCHIO,
TRANS. & INTROD.
The Southern Question
Vol. 5, Social Criticism, $5.00

DANIELA GIOSEFFI
Word Wounds and Water Flowers
Vol. 4, Poetry, $8.00

WILEY FEINSTEIN
Humility's Deceit: Calvino Reading
Ariosto Reading Calvino
Vol. 3, Criticism, $10.00

PAOLO A. GIORDANO, ED.
Joseph Tusiani: Poet, Translator,
Humanist
Vol. 2, Criticism, $25.00

ROBERT VISCUSI
Oration Upon the Most Recent Death
of Christopher Columbus
Vol. 1, Poetry, $3.00

Published by BORDIGHERA, INC., an independently owned not-for-profit scholarly organization that has no legal affiliation to the University of Central Florida, The John D. Calandra Italian American Institute, or State University of New York—Stony Brook.